CHANNING GARDNER

Don't Be A Lemon

No one wants to buy a lemon car and No one wants to follow a lemon leader.

This book was professionally typeset on Reedsy.
Find out more at reedsy.com

DEDICATED TO:

For those that I am blessed to lead.
You are what makes me a better leader.

My Why:
I am a shield to those God allows me to lead. I am meant to lead
many not few.

Contents

Acknowledgement

I have to start by thanking my wonderful husband, Ben. The support you provided from reading early drafts to giving me advice on the cover kept me going. Without your confidence in me, this book would not have been possible. Thank you for putting up with my wild imagination.

Thank you to my friends and family who read the book and gave me honest feedback to help me create a book that I feel enormous amounts of pride in. Your advice helped me to improve key areas of the book and maintain the passion behind the words.

I give full credit for the knowledge that I've gained and the vision for this book to God. I'm so thankful that I was trusted with this task and given the skills to complete it. I will continue to be obedient to the callings placed on my heart and steward the projects that have been assigned to me.

May we never grow tired of doing good.

Leadership

There is a misconception about leadership that is pervasive in our society. It is taught by the education system and by the role models that we have growing up. We've been told our entire childhood and much of our adult lives that leadership is an authoritative position. It has been ingrained in our brain presets by repetitive modeling of adults and authoritative figures. The problem is, this principle is simply not true.

Leadership is an influence position.

Consider the celebrities in Hollywood. They have no authority over anyone, yet they persuade millions around the world because of their influence. What do they persuade? Celebrities influence people's purchase decisions with fashion & beauty products. They can raise millions of dollars for causes. They bring billions to the movie industry just for being listed in the film. And most of the time, they forget that with great influence comes great responsibility.

I believe that with enough push and education, we can correct the mindset. It's time to start teaching the true realities and characteristics of an effective leader. You have to make it your mission to develop as a leader for the benefit of those you lead, not yourself. Don't be a lemon leader. I encourage you to look at this book as a study guide. It is meant to be interactive with your life. Each time you pick it up, you will likely lean into a new chapter more than you did before. If you allow this book to guide you on your leadership journey, I know that you'll find yourself growing year over year.

My name is Channing Gardner and I am a wife, mother, and insurance agency owner in the great state of Oklahoma. I lead a team of 45 insurance agents nationwide with members of my team ranging in experience; from brand new agents to those with years in the business. I was a leader for 15 years on the competitive cheer squad that I was a part of. I was one of the only teen moms at my high school who stayed after becoming pregnant to graduate. I strive to be the best at everything that I take on in life. Leadership is no different. During this book, you will get to know me through my mistakes and self-corrections in leadership. I hope that you'll be able to take the lemons from my mistakes and make lemonade in your organization.

Have you ever heard the saying "lemon car"? In simple terms, any nonconformity, defect, or a combination of defects that substantially impair the safety, use, or value of a new vehicle, constitutes a lemon. Basically, it looked like a good car, but in fact, it was not. It is the same with leaders. Some people "look the part", but don't have the skills or are unwilling to learn the skills to lead effectively. This book tackles how you can avoid being a lemon leader. Because no one wants to buy a lemon car and no one wants to follow a lemon leader.

Leadership is a servant position, not a selfish position. I'm going to argue that leadership is not a position at all, but rather a set of characteristics that a person displays and models consistently. This is where so many leaders go wrong. Lemon leaders focus their attention on what everyone else is doing wrong or they push their agenda on those they lead. You cannot force a vision. However, you can force a task.

For instance, I have a vision of a nonprofit that offers support, empowerment, and teaches life skills to teen mothers. That is the vision. I need to surround myself with other people who share the same passion and vision. I can require people to complete tasks to make the mission happen, but I can't force a belief in the vision. I have to inspire people to get their buy-in on the mission. If I can do that well, I won't need to force the tasks to be done. The people around me will volunteer because of their faith in the vision. Your vision is the lighthouse that keeps your team focused and guides them away from complacency.

Maybe it's better posed with questions.

Are you working on a mission or a task?

Is your goal going to make a difference?

Does the difference only affect you or does it lead to a positive outcome for a larger group?

Are you trying to make a difference in the world, or are you working for the power and glory of an ego-driven mission or task?

A well-defined vision will inform all of your tasks and actions. It will be the foundation that you build your plans. Your decisions should be based on how they affect the attainment of the specific goal. If everyone in your organization understands this simple vision, then you have done enough to move the mission forward. The closer that your organization relates to your vision, the faster you are likely to hit and exceed any goals that you've set for yourself and your team. A team without a vision-focused leader is like a boat without a lighthouse. The boat could potentially make it safely to dock.

> *Wouldn't it be easier, more effective, and safer guided by the beam of a lighthouse?*

When I was in my first leadership role professionally, I was not prepared for it. That is simply because I'd never studied leadership before. I didn't consistently display or act in a way that a true leader would. I believed the saying, "fake it until you make it." I can honestly say that I think this is one of the most destructive sayings. It implies very negative things.

1) I am not qualified to be in the position that I'm in.

2) If I succeed, it is likely due to luck rather than competence.

3) I have no confidence in my abilities so my team shouldn't either.

4) I'm not being intentional with my actions or tasks. *"Faking it" is not the same as studying or intentionally improving a skill.*

How could anyone be successful in a position if they haven't learned the skills that will be required of them daily? Now, that doesn't mean that you wait until you are 100% ready either. It means that you take on new roles and tasks with intentionality and honesty in where you're falling short. Only by these two things can you gain the necessary knowledge and skills.

I went into leadership only looking out for myself. I was worried about my income, my goals, my tasks, and my numbers. Looking back, it is not shocking to me at all that I did not accomplish any of the goals that I had set for myself and my team. I was not being a leader, nor was I taking any actionable steps towards becoming a better leader. I was being a dictator. And worse, I was one with little knowledge.

I kept failing in the same areas. I'd recruit an agent, sell them on the dream and get their buy-in on the possibilities of a career in our organization. Then, I would fail as a leader when it came to daily tasks and motivation. Inevitably, they would lose their faith in the mission and leave. I'd then repeat the process all over again and wonder what was wrong with the people I was recruiting. Never looking to myself for being the problem.

There was one agent I recruited who had a lot of potential. He was sharp, well-educated, and kind. I was very impressed by how quickly he could learn and retain new information. Although he had no experience, you wouldn't know it from his actions or the confidence he had in himself. He was so excited to begin his career in the field and had full "buy-in" on the vision of the organization. During his first week in the agency, he had some personal things happen which led to him starting his career slower than either of us had hoped. Rather than being sympathetic to the situation and helping him in whatever way I could, I wasn't the leader I should have been. I took away his leads and gave them to someone else, I checked in daily for my purposes instead of making sure he was okay, and because of my actions I wasn't able to repair the relationship. He left quickly and never returned.

I held no ownership of the issues I was facing. That is not leadership. It was a disservice to myself and more importantly, it was a disservice to those I was supposed to lead. I had people who were relying on me to be their lighthouse and help them accomplish their dreams. Instead, I lead them into a defeated mindset. I was not adequately prepared for the position because I was not learning how to lead effectively.

Once I realized this, I very quickly changed my focus from what everyone else was doing wrong to what I could be doing better. I went back to the drawing board. That is when I learned that leadership requires a purpose. Your vision will inform everything else you do. This time around, I met with my team and we laid out a clear and defined path with checkpoints for success. Those checkpoints created micro-goals so that the team could celebrate small victories. A pie is much easier to eat one slice at a time. And guess what? We had a higher rate of success. It also allowed the team to rest periodically so we didn't burn out.

Influence is a larger responsibility than authority.

If someone has authority without influence, they won't move people into action. This means that their organization or team will remain stuck in the same situation regardless of the leader's efforts, a perpetual state of passivity. If the team remains stagnant, the leader won't have a negative effect on those they lead because they will have no influence at all. If someone has influence, it is impossible to not have authority. Their influence will drive people to action. The people who they influence are choosing to follow rather than being commanded to follow. That is where true power comes from. True power is earned and given freely not taken by command. That is the nature of influence.

Influence originates from purpose.

Once you discover your purpose, establishing an intimate connection with it will provide a solid foundation for your leadership ability. Your desire to become a better leader should stem from an innate understanding that you are needed and you can make a difference for the world around you, including those you lead.

The skill of influence is largely a communication skill.

Learning how to effectively communicate not just what you want the outcome to be, but why. Influence is inspiring your people to move in unison so that the goal can be accomplished. How much more effective would your team be if they were all pushing to accomplish the same goal?

First, you must create an environment that is focused on assisting everyone rather than assisting a few. Leadership is the most individualized team sport that you can be a part of. Your team needs to move together towards a common goal, but each teammate has to hold themselves accountable at the same time. Imagine that your actions alone can't solve the problem, but your actions alone can escalate or create the problem.

The entire team needs to get behind the mission for maximum

effectiveness. Therefore, moving an entire force to a single finish line. Sure, you can try to do it on your own, but it will be easier to accomplish with a group of like-minded people. Your team can also help to motivate you when you're feeling overwhelmed or exhausted. You are also responsible for reciprocating that when your team needs it.

Every member of your team has strengths and weaknesses. You can better utilize their skills by knowing about their individual specialties. Think about their strengths and weaknesses as pieces to a puzzle that must be placed to solve the issue at hand. Authoritative leaders don't always place teams strategically. Influential leaders consider where each member of the team would be the most effective at moving the mission forward.

> *True authority comes from leading willing followers who have full confidence and trust in their leader.*

It takes time to get there. It takes intentional effort to earn the right to lead willing followers. It takes proving yourself daily to your team, showing them you're worthy of their faith and attention. When you take the time to learn how to communicate more effectively, it will increase your influence. Taking time to get to know your people on a more personal level will help you understand how each person prefers their communication to be delivered. Trust me, I don't have the same communication style as many of my agents or my husband. It is up to you to learn how to effectively communicate with each person that you have a relationship with.

I used to bark orders at agents when they behaved in a way that I did not agree with or that didn't help move our mission forward. Then, surprise, I had no agents. I've taken time to get to know my leadership style. I know that I'm zero to sixty miles per hour leader. I need permission from my team to lead them hard. Until I get their permission, I can't be effective when our backs are up against the wall. Getting their permission to lead hard allows me to be their partner in the mission, but also drive the train when we go off the rails. Since I've implemented the permission rule, our agency retention has doubled.

Will we be able to maintain every agent because of the changes that have been made?
    No.

Will every person give their permission to be led hard?
    No.

Will the team have a better shot at success if we can identify who can take tough leadership and who needs to be handled with kid gloves?
    Yes.

You can't pretend that you have all the answers, because it will damage your credibility and create a toxic culture. Having the humility to learn from others is admirable for any leader. You might feel like you know everything when your team is depending on you, but that couldn't be further from the truth. No one likes a know-it-all. The best leaders are those who make an effort to learn from their mistakes and grow from the knowledge they've gained, even if it means having a little humility.

Don't be afraid to ask for help or reassign tasks that you're not equipped to handle on your own. You might think that your team is depending on you to know everything. But it comes back to this idea that I keep talking about: Your team is made up of individuals with different strengths and weaknesses. So, why would you handle every problem or task on your own?

You might also find it helpful to show or share with your team some of the things that inspire you as a leader. Your team needs to know that you're on the same side, even if they might never understand some of your decisions. I have found great inspiration in seeing my leaders learn, grow, and empower their teams so I am compelled to do the same.

The more you can understand your team and what motivates them, the easier it will be to deliver a message that is heard and understood. That's why communication skills are paramount as a leader. Trust takes time to build, but it can be destroyed quickly. When your team feels like they're not listened to or like they don't have a voice, they'll start to become numb. They won't care about their work or the vision, which will end up causing more communication issues down the road. Remember, All good communication comes from good listening.

If you aren't inspiring change or action, you're just not delivering the right message.

Now you can see how important it is to get to know the communication style of those you lead. This doesn't mean that you walk on eggshells around your people. In fact, it does the opposite. It allows you to lead more effectively, get tough when you need to, and be empathetic when the time calls for it.

If someone's outlook on the goals or company changes, you pushed in a way that has caused resentment. You didn't listen to their wants and needs. You didn't communicate in their persuasion language. If you aren't hitting targets, you're not influencing focus within your team. It could also mean that you've lost track of the vision which is causing a roller coaster of production. It is likely, that you don't know your "why" and without a "why", it's impossible to know if you're on track or not.

My Why:
I am a shield to those God allows me to lead. I am meant to lead many, not few.

Every action I take is centered around that purpose. If it does not increase my ability to lead more people or to lead more effectively, I don't waste my time. I am singularly focused on growing and developing other leaders. Can you imagine what you'd be able to accomplish if you put all of your energy and attention into a singular item? I can guarantee that you would shock yourself with the results.

When you put a larger purpose behind your goal it also helps keep that fire alive. Now you're not just working towards an outcome that benefits you, but you have others relying on you to follow through. I find that I lead the best when I'm in the center of a team that's working together in unison towards something huge.

So far, we have been able to discuss some of the many aspects that make up a good leader. It's not enough just to be a "boss" and give orders – it takes courage, integrity, empathy, and more than anything else: self-awareness. Leaders must take responsibility for their actions as well as those of their team members. This is why leadership can sometimes be exhausting – you are responsible for your team in all areas of life! To do so successfully, leaders need to know how they react under pressure, faced with challenges, or setbacks. And most importantly: being a leader requires bravery from within yourself first before you can reach outward toward others who want guidance on their path.

In this book, we are going to break down the needed characteristics to be an effective leader. The great thing is, that all of these skills can be learned. The more that you model these skills, the quicker they will become habits. I encourage you to be brutally honest with yourself. If you've got the courage, ask for feedback from your team as well. Remember, the more ownership and blame that you take, the more that you can control the change and outcome.

Discipline

Discipline: *verb*
  train oneself to do something in a controlled and
  habitual way.

The first characteristic of leadership that we are going to dive into is discipline. Fitting, because this is the skill that you'll need to make long-term improvements in any area of leadership. Discipline is meant to build strength, not to be "fun" the entire time. It is the sacrifices that you are making today for a better tomorrow. The more that you practice discipline, the easier many areas of your life will become.

I tested my discipline by deciding to read the entire Bible within sixty days. Every. Single. Verse. I will be honest with you just as I expect you to be honest with yourself as you read along.

Confession #1: I can honestly say that I'm not a fan of Genesis.

90% of the book of Genesis is just a family tree that is difficult to keep up with, to be frank. But I continued with daily discipline because there is a greater purpose behind this exercise. I was training my brain and my body to become more disciplined. I know that just around the corner, there will be a lesson that needs to be learned or re-learned and because of this exercise, I'll now be ready.

I'm astonished at the changes in my thinking just from this seemingly simple exercise. The benefits of discipline are so worth it even when you don't feel like doing it. That's kind of the point of discipline in the first place. Notice how no one says that they are practicing discipline with the things they are naturally good at or enjoy doing from start to finish?

Let me clarify discipline even further. Discipline is not something that you can turn off and on like a switch. It's the daily act of doing what you know needs to be done even when you don't want to do it. For instance, working out at the gym, drinking the proper amount of water daily, or quitting bad habits that procrastinate your success. These are all acts of discipline. I'll be honest, I'm not the most disciplined when it comes to healthy habits, so this is definitely a principle that I will be consistently working on for the rest of my life. Imagine that. I need to be disciplined at being disciplined.

Let's get back to my Bible exercise. Within three days of beginning my Bible reading journey, I was already getting burnt out. How pathetic right? Here I am, supposed to be a leader in my organization, for my children, in the church and I can't even consistently read the bible for a week.

Would it be easier to quit or take a break?

What kind of character would that be building?

What kind of example does that set for my kids or those I lead?

Discipline isn't doing things until it becomes difficult and then allowing yourself to give up. Discipline is continuing to do things even when it is difficult. Without discipline, nothing great in life can ever be achieved. The point of my Bible exercise was to train myself. Learn to search for lessons in everything. Grow to be more patient. Accept that I won't enjoy every activity that I come across. Push through and build up stamina on mundane tasks. All the while, gaining more knowledge and getting a bird's eye view of some Bible principles I've been taught my whole life.

I'm sure that you get the point by now, but if not let me ask you this question: "Would you rather be disciplined every day or fail?" Because that is what it comes down to. You might see yourself in one or more of these scenarios below and think I can't relate. Trust me, I've been there too!

1. You want to start a business but you keep waiting for the "perfect time" to take action. Are you willing to wait until your life is perfect before you do anything? If you are, ask yourself when that will be exactly. Because let's be honest. You might not live long enough to see it. Or, the rest of the success in your life is waiting on the success of your business that you're waiting to start.

2. You want to lose weight but you keep waiting for the "perfect time" to start exercising or finding the "right gym" to join. So, let's think about that. You plan to wait until the stars align just right, then that will be when you start your exercise regime and membership? How perfect is

that timing going to be exactly?

3. You want to get a professional license but you keep waiting for the "perfect time" to enroll in the coursework. Have you ever heard of online study guides, online exams, or even temporary licenses that are available? What if this is the first step that you need to take for other doors to open for you?

The point is, that these are not valid excuses. There is no such thing as the perfect time! You just need to stop procrastinating and start practicing some discipline. Each of the scenarios above is very real within my own experience. I finally realized that it was time to stop making excuses and start training myself by practicing discipline.

Confession #2: I wanted to quit leading more times than I'd like to admit.

I've been training myself to bet on my talents, to grow in leadership, and to take myself and my success seriously. There have been days that I did not even want to get out of bed because even thinking about the tasks ahead of me made me tired. But no matter what, every day you have a new opportunity for growth or complacency.

Which one do you choose?

Our society teaches us that when the going gets tough, it's okay to walk away. And what a shame that truly is. I've heard talk about the 1% of Americans that are wealthy beyond comprehension. Everyone wants to be them, but few would make the same sacrifices to get there. Most people of the 1% club all have one thing in common. Discipline. They are not easily swayed off a task. They hyper-focus until their goal is accomplished.

Would you keep going even if it seemed impossible, difficult, or pointless?

The fact is the wealthy and successful don't accept defeat. They keep driving forward even when it seems hopeless. They have a relentless belief that they can accomplish their dreams if they have the discipline to keep going. It's easy to quit when we do not see immediate results in our effort. This is especially true in leadership and with the following:

What if I can't help everyone?

What if my leadership, encouragement, or training does not make an impact on them?

What if they don't respond to what I say?

I would challenge adding one additional question into your self-doubt.
   What if I succeed?

This has been an area of growth for me. Our industry can be compared to planting a garden, watering it, and then waiting for the fruits to come up. I too have been guilty in thinking that if I don't see immediate results or responses, then what is the point? This mindset has cost me countless opportunities to give my input on building character in other potential leaders. Because I was not disciplined enough to be present daily for them, I lost the opportunity to lead some, others grew slower than was possible, and the organization as a whole suffered for it.

When I began my career in life insurance, it came very naturally to me. I'll be honest most things in my life have. That is not me bragging. Because, since things have come easily to me, I've rarely had to practice discipline. That is why this is a skill that I will have to be intentional about my whole life. When I started my life insurance career, I was a top producer within the first few weeks. I was promoted to a supervisor position in just one and a half months. The promotion didn't make me nervous at all as I've always held leadership roles.

I failed to see that I would need years of development to handle the type of leadership role that I found myself in. I shouldn't have accepted the position that quickly. It required more knowledge and skills than I had at the time for the new industry I had started.

Did I know how to lead?
Sure, in specific situations.

Was I equipped with the skills I would need to succeed in this role at the time I accepted it?
No.

Could I obtain the information through practicing discipline and intentional daily effort?
Yes.

Previous to this point in my life, I had always been a leader on my competitive sports teams. As I soon found out, leading professionals is completely different. I imagined a world where everyone wanted to follow me and I was able to influence hundreds of people into doing the tasks that I deemed necessary. Within two months of my promotion, I had lost everyone. I ran everyone off because of my gaps in leadership effectiveness. No agents. No one to the left to lead, except myself.

I blamed everyone else, saying, "they aren't coachable. They don't want to learn. Or, they won't take direction." It took me months to realize that the people I was tasked with leading weren't the problem. The issue was me. I was not an effective leader. If I was to be successful, I needed to cram as much leadership and communication knowledge as quickly as possible and learn to implement it immediately. There are now endless resources for learning the skills of leadership. It takes discipline to implement one skill at a time until you become effective in each skill. I found that focusing on one skill at a time allowed me the ability to truly grasp each characteristic that I needed to gain. By practicing discipline with each skill, my leadership abilities greatly improved.

I'm told that we live in a generation of instant gratification and immediate results. So what does this mean for people like me – those who desire growth? It means we must put forth the effort every single day to see the results we want. The consequences for not doing so could be life-altering or damaging.

A quick example: Only a few weeks ago, I was reflecting on my discipline of reading the Bible. That goal was a short-term goal. But, as I look back over the last year, I've read my Youversion Bible app every day since. I've completed over 100 guided devotions and now lead several of my agents on weekly devotionals. Our group posts a verse of the day to encourage our organization.

That seemingly unimportant exercise of reading the full Bible in 60 days, gave me the discipline to keep reading, the confidence to share, and the personal growth in leadership skills along the way. Don't give up, keep going! You will see results if you stay the course and continue to apply discipline. I'm now aware of the power of intentional work ethic and discipline every day. The benefits are life-changing. I've experienced it myself. Will you? It's important to note - in all contexts - that you must be a good follower before you can become a good leader. This means not only taking responsibility for actions but also acknowledging when others have fallen short and encouraging the necessary change for the benefit of the organization.

Three of my favorite quotes ever:

I never lose. I either win or I learn.

Commitment has nothing to do with how you feel.

Lead, follow or get out of the way.

I've committed to my agency to grow as a leader, to serve my team, and to protect our community. I've committed to my family to provide a better living, practice my patience, and develop as a mother. I committed to finishing the Bible in sixty days. If I can accomplish one goal, what would stop me from tackling the next?

The choice is simple, keep pushing or give up and my "Mama didn't raise no quitter." Before focusing on growing as a leader, this was just pure stubbornness. That worked for a bit, but it takes being intentional, not prideful, to truly learn and implement new skills that aren't a natural talent. Failure is uncomfortable. Discipline will take the failures and turn them into turning points.

I've always believed that if I work hard enough, then I can accomplish anything. And while that still rings true today, after almost two decades of leadership, it's clear to me that the old adage is actually half-true. It's not just about working hard; you have to work smart, too.

Many things will happen to us in life. Most things will try and deter you from the path that you've committed to. It is imperative to *"just keep swimming"* to quote Dory from *Finding Nemo*.

Go back to the start.

Why did you originally make the commitment that you did?

What was the motivation behind the goal?

What did you hope to have accomplished by completing the task?

Can you learn to realize that you didn't fail, you were just learning?

Until you have the answers to these, you won't know what your next step is. These answers will show you if you need to change lanes and exit the highway for a new destination or if you just hit an unexpected road bump.

I have taken a long hard look at why I am in this career. There are other jobs out there that offer stable pay, better employee benefits, and a greater retirement plan; however, those jobs don't make me feel the passion that I feel for helping families and small businesses with security for the future. My career allows me to help people. I have the opportunity to make a difference in my community. That is what keeps me going every day.

Take pride in showing up to work each day and start your day with this question:

What can I do today that will help someone else?

Leadership is a skill. Discipline is a skill. Both must be carefully watched for effectiveness and areas of improvement. If we are not careful, that "break" or excuse will turn into the demise of the principles or skills we were trying to develop. And if that is allowed to happen, it halts any progress. Find a process for accountability that works for you. If you're anything like me, it is best to put goals with discipline. Break them down into micro-accomplishments so that you see the success on your way to the much larger task. Remind yourself that you are not losing. You are learning. And by continuing to face that head-on every day, your winning is inevitable.

It is also important to master each step to be truly, permanently effective in the new skill you've gained. The jack of all trades never got paid handsomely for knowing a little about a

22

lot. The specialist is the one who gets the paycheck. It is better, by this thought, to know a lot about a little. The great thing is, you can keep developing over time. Master one skill through discipline and then move on to mastering the next. Mastery of skills is what matters, not just the general knowledge of them. Patiently seek improvement rather than quickly demanding it. Small consistent steps are the key to success

Remember, you are all that lies between where you are today and where you want to be tomorrow. Keep your chin up, look forward with a determined expression on your face, but don't forget to enjoy each step along the way. Happiness is our most important component for growth because it keeps us focused.

To bring it all home, it would have been wise of me to hold off on the leadership position for a longer period of time. Not because I didn't want it, but because I wasn't a master of the necessary skills yet. How can I expect others to follow me when I don't know the task or job inside and out with full confidence? It also would have been easier for me to master the leadership role if I wasn't still developing my skills in sales. It's a double-edged sword.

At the time, I felt that if I turned down the leadership opportunity then I wouldn't be able to get another chance for a long time. The reality is, if I had truly mastered the skills needed, I would have naturally moved into the leadership role. I could have trained and helped more agents at my level and started to learn the leadership role before being placed in it. The fact is, I did it backward. Discipline would have served me well and accelerated my career at a faster velocity because of the mastery that I would have acquired in my skill set. First, you learn to follow, then you learn to lead.

If you are at that crossroads in your career, I encourage you to enjoy the bus stop you're at now. Appreciate the skills that you get to learn in your current position. Enthusiastically accomplish the tasks that you're responsible for. Search for new tasks to learn once you've accomplished your own. If you can't learn to follow, it will be impossible for you to lead. If you can't learn to lead, you might as well get out of the way because someone else is willing to make the sacrifices you are not.

Fight

Fight: *verb*
    endeavor vigorously to win.

We all have one opportunity that is equal in life. No matter what your background is, where you were raised, or what your living situation looked like. We all have the opportunity to fight. Fight for your family. Fight for your finances. Fight for your dreams. Fight for your value. There is a reason why we are instinctively designed with a "fight or flight" trigger. Too often people choose the flight option when things get tough even if their goals are achievable. All they have to do is just stand up and fight for them.

I have been in the fight of my life over the last five years. I have fought so hard to get out of debt, to escape mediocrity, and to earn a spot among the top earners in this country. Never forget that money doesn't always come easy. Sometimes you need to fight for it! I'm fighting for this vision because I know there are things God has called me to accomplish that will involve me volunteering much of my time. I'm fighting now to create the resources that I'll need in the future.

Fighting doesn't always mean that you get the outcome that you wanted.

Look at Kris Moutinho. If you're not familiar with who this is, he is an American UFC Fighter who had an epic fight on July 10, 2021, against Sean O'Malley. Before he became a UFC pro, Moutinho worked at a paint factory. He was making enough money to pay his bills, but he knew he was meant for more. He shifted into a singular focus and turned all his attention on his fighting career in June of 2020.

On July 10th, 2021 O'Malley was scheduled to fight Smolka, but Smolka was forced to withdraw from the fight last minute. Moutinho threw his name in the hat to fight O'Malley. He had no expectation of actually being selected. He was shocked when the opportunity was awarded to him with just 9 days left until the fight.

During his debut fight, Moutinho absorbed 230 significant strikes from O'Malley. 177 of those were shots to his head. That is the second-most for a three-round fight in the UFC franchise history. The "Green Zombie," as he would come to be known from his debut, became increasingly disfigured as hit after hit landed with precision to his face.

Moutinho couldn't match his opponent in strikes, but he did more. He brought heart, singular focus, and fight. He relentlessly pushed forward. Taking every hit and still pushing forward. Even to the very end, he fought. With 27 seconds left in the fight before the referee finally called the fight. Moutinho was willing to keep going and be punched in the face until the fight was completely finished. He even argued with the referee and begged to keep going through round four.

He lost the fight to O'Malley, but he gained something even

more precious. He won the respect of his opponent, was blasted into the spotlight, and has established himself in his dream industry. Moutinho may have lost the fight, but he still achieved a great victory. He won the right to continue fighting for his dreams without being judged by his new colleagues. He showed that he would never give up, even when faced with overwhelming odds. Countless people have chosen to fight in order to change their circumstances.

Too often the fight is set with the wrong enemy or adversary in mind. We fight with those we love or lead. We fight with ourselves. These are not the things that are causing the issues or hurdles that we face in life. Our loved ones and teams are actually the ones that can help us to conquer what stands in front of us. In fact, relying on those that can assist us will enhance the efforts that we are making toward our goals.

If you could cut the time to achieve your goals in half, would you do it?

Learn to transfer your fight from people and onto tasks. Fight to bring your true self forward. You don't have to be a fighter in the worldly sense, but fight to live as your true self and do what you love. Fight for those who can't fight for themselves. Fight against those things that are not right in this world - corruption, greed, hatred, etc.

Often times we avoid tasks that are not our strong suit. When we avoid things we struggle with, we actually handicap ourselves. If I avoided training other agents because it was not a strong suit of mine, I would then never learn how to train new agents. Seems pretty self-explanatory. If I never kicked a soccer ball with my left foot, I wouldn't be effective at kicking the soccer ball with half the feet that I have available. Do you see the handicap that would be solidified? Fight the tasks that you struggle with until you no longer struggle or at least you don't struggle as much.

Instead of avoiding the things that are difficult, learn to love the challenge. Put a game to it. If it takes you 20 minutes to complete a task, time yourself. Set a goal to learn to accomplish the task in 15 minutes.

What additional skills would you need to learn or master in order to accomplish your goal?

Is it effective to learn to be quicker at this task or does it cause the quality to suffer?

When do you want to be able to reduce the time the task takes you?

Don't be afraid to fail. Even if you are not successful on your first try, don't give up - allow yourself another chance at it until you can master it. If people were too afraid of failing they would never know what success felt like. I've come to realize that the only way that failure exists is by not even trying at all. You might be unsuccessful in your first attempt, but I challenge you to not look at that as a failure, but rather an area you can improve in. A skill you can fight for. Only if you never try, could you ever fail. Fight to be the best that you can be for yourself and those that depend on you. Most importantly, never give up on your dreams - EVER! Every single person has something to contribute and something of value to offer the world.

Fight for goals until you accomplish them. When you fight to improve your situation or your skill-set you need to commit to the discipline of learning. Don't be defeated by minor setbacks. Oftentimes, a setback tells you the goal is right around the corner. Life has a funny way of testing our tenacity. Those that push through and fight to accomplish the goals are rewarded with the completion of the goal. Those that give up and plan to "go back" to the task at a later date will realize they are right where they left off or even further behind. If you can be trusted with little, you will be given much.

If you haven't already, gather the tools and information you need to accomplish your goal. Know what success looks like and how it will be measured. Write down step-by-step, detail-by-detail what needs to happen to achieve that goal. Now fight yourself or those obstacles in your way with these tasks that you've set for yourself. When you get knocked down, get back up and fight again until your goal is complete.

We all have the same 24 hours in a day and the same freedom to fight. In my younger years, I chose to allow life to happen to me. I gave my circumstances full control. I lead when it was a situation that I was confident in and bowed out when I didn't feel I was worthy to lead. I had my son at 18 years old from an unpleasant situation. My son was at my high school graduation, which the school tried to talk me out of attending. I didn't feel fit to be a mother so I transferred that responsibility to my parents. I didn't know how to value myself so I gave others the right to label me how they wanted. I allowed myself to slowly be chipped away until there was very little of me left. I had lost myself. I didn't want to fight; I gave up and became a victim to the world.

Then one day, it was like a light bulb came on. Nothing

positive was happening because I wasn't fighting. I had given up. It will likely take me my whole life to complete the 180° that I need to make to become the mother, daughter, and leader I know that I'm capable of being now. I will fight for the rest of my life to become the person that I see myself being in the future. It is up to me and me alone to fight for the change in circumstances. It is up to me to take responsibility for myself and my life.

Since my "light bulb day," I began the fight of my life to improve my situation and skill-set little by little. It seemed like such a small effort at the time but it is that small effort that began my transformation. It has been a difficult journey to get where I am and I have so much further to go. It is likely that you have had a similar experience. Remember, when you find yourself lost in life or when things are tough, there is always an opportunity to get back up and fight some more.

The easier thing to do is to give up. To fold under the pressure. To continue to allow the world to label you based on past mistakes. I'd rather fight the rest of my life for the labels that I know I am in my heart.

I am:
  Advocate
  Confident
  Worthy
  Empathetic
  Influential
  Capable
  Loved
  Blessed
  Talented

Are you willing to take full responsibility for your successes and failures?

I hope you are.

Take some time to write some of the labels that you'd like to be known for.

What kind of legacy do you want to leave behind?

I am:

_____

_____

_____

_____

_____

_____

_____

Full ownership is the best way to fight. If I throw all the punches then I can choose where they land. It's a continuous journey for myself and for you as well. Find your fight and don't stop fighting. Don't allow the world to label you. It has no right. Find your core, remind yourself of it daily, and fight each day to make that your truth. No one will pay you to be a victim. Too many people now expect others to treat them as they see themselves in their heads. The total truth is no one is required to treat you in any particular way. You earn the right to a certain treatment. Unfortunately, you can earn positive treatment or negative treatment.

Can you handle the full responsibility of your accomplish-

ments and failures alike?

Leaders need to fight for victory every day because it's the only way to ensure lasting success for ourselves and our teams. The world is constantly changing and evolving, which means leaders can't afford to become complacent. They need to be constantly fighting for progress and innovation in order to stay ahead of the competition. Furthermore, leaders need to be fighting for their teams, empowering them to reach their full potential. When everyone is working together towards a common goal, then anything is possible. Victory is within reach if everyone is willing to fight for it!

Invest

Invest: *verb*
  devote (one's time, effort, or energy) to a particular undertaking with the expectation of a worthwhile result.

Everyone nowadays wants to invest. They invest in the stock market. They invest in a home. They invest in a car. They invest in their IRA. It seems ridiculous that people are so willing to invest in everything except for themselves and their relationships. Without investment in yourself and your relationships, you can't truly make an impact anywhere. One of my favorite sayings is,

> *"If you want to go fast, go alone. If you want to go far, go with others."*

For people to want to go with you, you have to be worthy. The best thing to do for increasing influence is to invest in yourself, your skill development, and your personal growth. No one becomes a legend overnight. No one accidentally gets to lead thousands of people successfully.

Successful leaders don't invest for a short while, they invest for a lifetime. A true leader has a schedule they stick to for self-development. You drive to work every day or you have a morning routine if you work from home. Turn that jam session you have on your commute to work into a session of leadership podcasts or principles. Find an audiobook or podcast that pumps you up, but also gives you useful information for you to implement quickly. I like to bounce around between audiobooks, the Bible, and podcasts. Keeping the topics focused on leadership or communication, but from different voices helps my stamina with the intake of information.

There was one month when I was particularly struggling. I had a rock star agent who was dependable, consistent, and always in a positive move. I was so proud when I got to introduce a promotion for the agent to a supervising position. After the promotion, that agent began to change. They would come in at seemingly random times throughout the day. Their sales took a nosedive. They became resentful and not pleasant to be in the office with. I was torn up about this. My first instinct was obviously to take it personally and believe that I was outside of any blame for the total personality transformation. But then, I began going to my Podcast Mentors for solutions to the agent's behavior.

What I found was not a solution that I would have thought of. I realized that the agent's actions were not their fault, but mine. I had pushed a leadership position on someone. They already were a leader in the organization, but a leadership position was not what they wanted. They had only accepted the position because they didn't want to let me down. They resented me for pressuring their decision because it added a lot of unwanted responsibilities to their plate. The change in their behavior was because I did not listen to them and their individual goals. That was my failure as a leader.

Because of the daily investment in leadership development, I was able to get a handle on the situation and correct my actions. I sat the agent down and began with an apology. I expressed how my actions were not looking out for their best interest and goals. I apologized for pushing a position on them they were not seeking. I offered to give them back their original position without any judgment as it was my mistake from the beginning. I asked if there was anything that I could do to correct the error that I had made in our relationship. Thankfully, the advice from my Podcast Mentors helped to mend the relationship and I now have my top producer back in full swing. Without investing in my development as a leader I would have certainly lost a great person, agent, and friend.

Self-development is the first key to true success. If I take the focus off of growing myself and turn it to constantly correcting others' behaviors around me, I will be the lid to my organization.

We have a saying on our team,

"Lead, follow, or get out of the way."

There are times when I need to step out of the way so that I am not the cause for issues within the agency. To be effective, you must be willing to sacrifice your time outside of work to develop yourself. It is the only way to get to a new desired destination.

You need to be obsessed with your progression. Self-development doesn't happen overnight. It is just like going to the gym. It takes consistency and obsession to truly become great. I look back at the leadership mistakes that I made just four months ago and am thankful for all the extra hours put into my self-development. You will be as well.

Are you determined to hit your targets?

Leaders often focus on targets of revenues, sales, or hires. These are all great targets. Without profit, you'd have no company. I challenge you to align your targets with growing in your leadership role as well. Set a target of the number of hours you pour into yourself on a daily or weekly basis. I'm not a huge proponent of set daily schedules, but I do have a checklist that I complete daily. On that checklist are items that the agency needs from me to produce income, but I also have daily tasks that I need to accomplish as a leader to grow for the agency and those that I lead.

It's completely acceptable to be relentless in building strong relationships. Society today is set up for immediate gratification. There isn't anything wrong with that necessarily. The key is learning to develop focus in particular areas of your life to keep going when "the going gets tough". Relationships are one of those areas. Leaders don't give up on relationships when they get tough. Leaders dig their heels in and work on that relationship even more. Make a commitment to yourself to not throw in the towel too early. It certainly would have been easier for me to blame my agent, not accept their behavior, and let them walk out the door. But, I made a commitment to myself to develop strong relationships.

In the end, is it truly "easier" starting over?

If you want to achieve the goals that you've set for yourself, you don't have the time to replace struggling relationships. You must believe that without strong people and relationships around you, it will cause your own destruction. Everyone needs people around them to keep them on the right track. These supporters should be pushing you when you're feeling unmotivated, encouraging you when you feel down, growing with you to increase your potential, and relying on you to drive the mission forward.

The fact is, without responsibility for others, you're not truly a leader. If you are not in a position right now where your title puts you in an authoritative position, that's okay. It doesn't take a title to be responsible for others. Learn to take initiative and pour into others regardless of a technical title that is given to you. Remember, leadership is earned not given. You've got a greater chance of being promoted into leadership when you lead from the middle.

The success of your relationships starts with you, not them. You're responsible for pouring into yourself so that you have the energy and knowledge to pour into them. To have the best relationships, you need to be the best version of yourself. Plain and simple. This means that you need to take in knowledge and utilize it daily. Simply learning the information is not enough. You need to implement that information as well.

Don't try to rush through the material. Take time to pause so your mind can fully take in the information. There are so many different topics that encompass leadership. Start with the two that are frustrating you the most. Or, the two you feel you need the most improvement in. Flip back and forth and repeat the same information back either out loud or by taking notes. Then move on to teach someone else the information.

Retention is 60% more effective when you utilize all of these techniques together.

When I was new to my leadership role, I can recall several times that I failed. The key area of my failures was not putting others first. Not leading from a place of service. I had an agent who found out she was pregnant. She had a very high-risk pregnancy. I also had another agent who struggled with epilepsy and was unable to drive most days because of it. Instead of sitting down with each agent individually and getting to know those struggles more in-depth, I made a blanket rule. It would have been very easy for me to design hours in the office that would work around their physical constraints and still lead to them being successful. Instead, I disregarded the relationship as an individual one and required them to follow the same rules as everyone. This obviously led to both agents leaving. If I had cared more about the relationships and built them stronger by being flexible, those strong agents would have stayed. I sacrificed both successful agents because I did not value them enough as individuals. I was a lemon leader

You're stronger when you're surrounded by others.

You should rely on those you trust for daily guidance, on your team for daily growth, and on other leaders for daily encouragement. It is often difficult to lean on others when you are also a leader. Especially if you are a leader who struggles with pride, like me. I've learned that I don't always need to be the "strongest" in the room.

It is more important that I have strong people around me.

They will step up and cover the gaps in my leadership without hesitation as long as I am the best leader that I can be for them. Better to be one—with many united for a common cause than to be many-with-one struggling to find a singular purpose to fight for.

Be selfish by investing in your self-development so that you can be selfish with growing strong, beneficial relationships. Find something that speaks to you; books, webinars, online training, podcasts, audiobooks, YouTube videos, motivational speeches, skills-based training, etc. Make it a point to create a habit of self-development daily for at least one to two hours per day. You'll be amazed where you are in 30 days. It is also helpful if you take time to journal. This will allow you to look back at your improvement and celebrate your successes, learn from your mistakes, and identify new areas you'd like to improve.

Personally, my journal looks like this:

1. One positive thing that happened that day.
2. What did I do to make that positive thing happen?
3. One negative thing that happened that day.
4. How did I make that negative thing happen?
5. Specific prayers, specific goals, and specific appreciations
6. Bible verse of the day personalized for my business

Your struggle points might continue to be there. The key is not to aim for perfection, but rather aim for daily growth. I know that I'm a better communicator with my team now than I was even just a month ago. I also know that I still make mistakes. Recognizing my downfalls will allow me to keep the interest high and continue to invest in myself. Take the tiny successes and focus on compounding them. Write out bullet points as to why those are labeled as successes to you.

Is it the action you took that causes it to be a considered a success?

Could you learn to take that course of action each time you're confronted with a similar situation?

Does your team agree that it was as successful as you believe it to be?

How can you improve on that success and yield an even greater return for next time?

Remember that to be successful in investing, you need to manage your risk rather than avoid it. You have made mistakes and you will make more. Investing in yourself is the best way to minimize the risk for the future and compound your interest by developing yourself and your relationships. Invest the time now to get the growth back in the future. Don't worry if you slip and miss a few days or say the wrong things. Investing in yourself is a constant journey, not a three-week training session. You should look at investing as a life-long adventure.

It is not typical in our society any longer to "stick with" something. Don't shy away from developing yourself. Others might not understand it. And that's okay. It is your mission to become the leader that you see yourself as. That will take your determination to blaze past the naysayers and create a life of constant learning. It is not a waste of your time. It is an investment in your future. It is an investment in the team you are leading or the future team you will lead later. Invest in yourself first always so that you can later invest in others.

Mission-Focused

Mission: *noun*
   a strongly felt aim, ambition, or calling.

Focus: *verb*
   pay particular attention to.

Let's start with a question.

If you've never failed, how would you know if you're succeeding?

I am a firm believer that without failure there can be no success. There is a bitter-sweet thing that comes from every failure. We learn. That is if we choose to. If you look at the stories we've covered so far you can see this prominent everywhere. I failed as a leader and chose to learn how to be better. Moutinho lost his first UFC physical fight but learned how to fight for his dreams to a level no other fighter has done yet. You've failed at numerous things, positions, or tasks, but you've picked up this book showing that you're willing to learn.

It seems these days that people are scared of failure, which leads them to not take the necessary risks. And that's a shame. If you're paralyzed by the fear of failure, there is no possibility for any success. It doesn't mean that we have to repeat the same mistakes constantly. If we choose to allow this to happen our growth has stopped. Failure is not the issue. Acceptance of failure is the real dream killer.

What if, instead, we all leaned into failure?

Decide to seek out failing at tasks. Remember, if we avoid all of the things that are not our strong suit something tragic happens. We remain handicapped by these shortcomings. Leaning into failure allows more room for growth. Think of failure as a slingshot. If you lean into a slingshot slightly, you'll still move forward. Now, use the full stretch of the slingshot. Lean all the way in and now it can propel you light years ahead of just casually resting into it. Running theme; get intentional. Life is too short and your mission is too important to casually "try" things out. Search out the areas that you are lacking and lean fully into the development of those areas.

What if we took the time to evaluate our failures?

Now that you've identified areas that you have failed in or situations that escaped your control, it's time to evaluate. Look at your top three failures. Track the action steps that you took leading up to the failure. Write down the responses that you had to the failure. Identify key areas of improvement that are fully in your control. Congratulations! Now you have the power to make adjustments to your response, skills, or knowledge to avoid continuously making the same mistake. The only loop you should be on is the loop to success. The fact is once you've got a handle on your shortcomings, the path to success is inevitable.

What if we learned something from every failure?

If we willingly chose to do this exercise with every failure, society would be much further along. This exercise can be done with people, on tasks, on communication, or inventions and processes. When we seek out answers to our mistakes, we can take corrective actions. Completing this exercise, we must focus on how the failure is because of us, not because of others. The fact is we can't control other people. We can influence them, but that takes us understanding what happened in the first place. Chances are, if you're in a leadership position and your team fails, you had a major hand in the failure even if you don't see it at first glance. Be relentless with seeking your faults. This list is not to drag you down, but the opposite. It is designed to build you up and give you the power to make a difference.

> Failure is not a consistent state unless you allow it to be.

If I look at a failure as a fault of me or a break in the process that I have control of, it gives me the ability to correct the issue, learn new skills, and adapt my method. If there is no ownership there can be no long-lasting solution. Even if you're leading from the middle, a failure is an opportunity for growth. I would argue to say that growth always begins with failure.

The cold hard fact is I need to fail. You need to fail. Your team needs to fail. Everyone everywhere needs failure. I need to fail every day and learn to be okay with it. As long as I am learning from those failures, am I not at the same time succeeding? When you no longer fear failure and instead get encouraged by it, your growth will be impossible to stop.

If you're in sales you can understand this principle. Every day, you make calls. When you make calls, you get rejected. The more rejections you get, the better you get at handling the rejection. The better you get at handling the rejections, the less rejection you get. The less rejection you get, the more clients you get to set with. The more clients you set with, the more practice you get on your presentation. The better you get at your presentation, the more deals you get to close. The more deals you close, the more money you make. So let's say that your goal is to make more money.

Do you not agree that you'd have to fail along the way?

If you sought out the failure at an accelerated speed would you not also reach your goal sooner because you've also accelerated your learning and growth?

Thus is life. Failure is essential to life and growth.

Time to lean hard into failure. Don't turn from the opportunity to learn. Time to learn fast from mistakes. Don't reject the coaching, training, or guidance of the leaders you rely on. And, my friends, it's also time to succeed. Don't rob yourself of the opportunity to realize your dreams and goals coming true.

I say all of this to bring us to our next essential characteristic of leadership. Being 100% mission-focused. If we can learn to disregard the fear of failure because it will inevitably be on our path, it allows us to pour our focus and energy into the completion of our mission. Everyone's mission looks a little different. I would rather spend my time moving the needle forward on something that I'm passionate about instead of giving my time and energy to fear. Wouldn't you? Create a space for yourself to dig in deep and find your mission. I recommend you go through this process to discover what is possibly hidden within you. I've adapted this from an experience I had at church. If you want a look at my real-life mission board, you can see each of these steps illustrated at https://www.channinggardne r.com/findyourmission

You'll need the following supplies; four different colors of sticky notepads, poster board (or space on a blank wall), and a pen.

Step One:
  Identify the people, events, and circumstances that have most affected your life. Write each of these down on one color sticky note. Use a separate sticky note for each one. Don't worry about sticking them anywhere yet.

Step Two:
  Put things into order. Create vertical rows, starting on the left. Arrange your sticky notes in chronological order. Place your earliest sticky note with enough space for sticky notes to go above and below.

Step Three:

Call it like it was. Identify the sticky notes that were painful or difficult when you experienced them. Rewrite each of those things on your second color sticky note and throw away the original sticky note that you're replacing

Step Four:

Organize your timeline into chapters. Look at the notes assembled on your page and organize them into chapters. Write a chapter title for each row on your third sticky note color. Place these chapter titles along the top of your columns.

Step Five:

Clarify the major lessons. Review your chapter titles and your other colored sticky notes under each chapter to see what major lesson emerges. Write these lessons on your fourth sticky note color and place them along the bottom of each column. Try to identify at least one lesson for each chapter. If you're struggling to identify major lessons, then ask yourself these questions

What was God trying to teach me during this chapter of my life?

What should I remember as I move forward?

What abilities or insights have been deposited into my life as a result of this experience

In what ways can the skills or insights I got through this experience impact my future?

What character traits did I develop as a result of this experience?

What character traits have I come to value most in others?

Are there any unique experiences or insights that I've gained?

What are some of the ways God has used me?

Did this experience reveal anything to me?

Rather than looking at your past experiences as things that happened to you, mold them into your mission. Reframe them. Ask yourself instead:

What was the point?

Why did that happen?

Where am I supposed to go from here?

How can I turn these lemons into lemonade?

What is my mission?

You are here for a reason. I don't believe that you've gone through what you've been through for no reason. Whether you've experienced tragedy or not, you've learned lessons. Those lessons are meant to be passed on to others. You've got great things to accomplish. By going through this exercise, my hope for you is that if you didn't already know what your purpose is, you will. Focusing on your mission will allow you to take the right steps at the right time and be able to define your success more clearly.

Humility

Humility: *noun*
   a modest or low view of one's own importance;
   humbleness.

Humility is a necessary skill for any leader to possess to help move their people to action. It is one of the greatest strengths that a leader can show to those they lead. It demonstrates that the leader is confident enough in their own abilities to put the needs of others before their own. Humble leaders are also more likely to be open to feedback and willing to learn from their mistakes. This allows them to constantly improve their skills and become even better leaders. If the leader stops growing and improving, the organization is likely to become stagnant.

There are many different types of humility, however, none is more important than self-effacing humility. Self-effacing humility involves demonstrating that your own needs and desires are less important than those of others. People who act humble in this way put the needs of their team above their own by making decisions that benefit others rather than themselves, even if it means making sacrifices in their time or interests.

Self-effacing humility is difficult for people to master because it runs counter to common human traits. A desire for self-promotion, attention, and credit are all driven by the ego; these desires resist humbling oneself in front of others. However, leaders who successfully develop this type of humility will attract and retain the most talented people, and therefore be able to push ahead with what they want to be done even more quickly than if they were working alone.

> There is no clear path to developing self-effacing humility as it involves constantly challenging human nature.

However, there are some things that leaders can try. One way to help develop self-effacing humility is to emphasize that you are part of the team that is working together to achieve something. This will help you to put your own desires aside for the benefit of everyone involved. It will also force you to be less focused on yourself and more focused on the goals of the team.

Being open about your weaknesses and mistakes is an important part of humility. If people know where they stand it allows them to support you better. By being honest with your team about your capabilities, you are admitting that you are not perfect and that you need help from others. This will make them more likely to want to help you and support you as a leader. It is those people who are closest to us that can see areas of improvement that we might not be able to see ourselves. Being open to hearing constructive criticism will speed up your leadership development significantly. Likewise, your followers need to know that the criticism will be taken without punishment or lashing back out at them.

One of the most important things that you can avoid doing is comparing yourself to others. It is also important not to set a standard for humility that is impossible to maintain. Give yourself some grace as you learn and develop these new skills. Trying to be as humble as someone else will only lead to disappointment and frustration. Instead, focus on developing your own unique brand of humility that works for you and makes you happy. People only want to follow leaders who are authentic. This builds trust. Trust brings forward momentum.

Focus on being humble in your own circumstances and do not worry about how others are acting or what they have achieved. Remember that everyone has their own strengths and weaknesses, and there is no need to compare yourself to others. Focus on being the best leader that you can personally be, and let your followers judge the success of your leadership based on their own individual experiences. Every single person has a part to play on the team for your organization. If you only focus on your weaknesses, your strengths are likely to diminish. If you focus only on your strengths, you cannot grow to your full potential. However, there are skills that a leader might not ever need to know about specific daily operations. Allow your team to fill in the gaps so that you can focus on more forward-moving tasks for the team. Strive for growth, not perfection.

Remember, that it's okay to ask for help from those around you as long as you don't expect them to solve problems for you. Leaders who try to do everything themselves will quickly become overwhelmed and ineffective. Instead, humble leaders rely on the skills and expertise of those around them to help get the job done. By asking for help, leaders can focus on their own strengths and weaknesses and become even more effective in the long run.

What tasks are on your plate that should be reallocated to someone else?

What are tasks that you've assigned to other members of your team that need to be put back onto your plate?

At the end of each day, do you feel like you didn't accomplish everything you needed to?

Humility is a difficult trait to develop, but it's one of the most important skills that a leader can have. It serves as an opportunity for leaders to show others that they are willing to put their own interests aside in order to achieve what is best for everyone involved. The best leaders will find ways to develop this skill within themselves, even if it means challenging the way they are naturally inclined to act. By developing humility, leaders will become better able to understand their followers and how best to lead them to success.

If a leader is unwilling to listen to feedback, they may be less able to understand the needs of their followers. This could lead to a lack of trust and communication, which would ultimately hinder the leader's ability to achieve their goals. The last thing you should be is the lid for your organization.

When I took the leadership position in insurance, I was extremely lacking in humility. I knew that I did not know everything, but I was unwilling to admit that to myself or my team. I was the lid of our organization. My lack of humility caused the entire production of the team to be affected because

I would not ask for help. I suffered and struggled for months. The worst part is, that I made my team suffer and struggle for months with me. If I had reached out for help prior to sinking as low as I allowed us to go, our team might have been able to retain more agents. We probably could have hit more of our production goals. Ultimately, the organization would have been better off as a whole. I had to realize that being humble and asking for help did not mean defeat. In fact, it meant that I was a stronger leader.

Many humble people can be open about their weaknesses and mistakes. By doing this, leaders show the people they lead that it is okay to make mistakes and that everyone makes them at some point. Leaders who are willing to admit where they need to improve are more likely to get followers because other people will see how human the leader is. It can be easy for followers to believe that their leader is above mistakes, but it's actually more effective if the person in charge admits where they went wrong.

One of the best ways to hold yourself accountable is to understand your current core values. Grab a highlighter and highlight every core values that you feel applies to you.

- Accountability
- Authenticity
- Boldness
- Collaboration
- Compassion
- Confidence
- Courage
- Creativity

- Dedication
- Devotion
- Discipleship
- Discovery
- Diversity
- Efficiency
- Encouragement
- Endurance
- Enthusiasm
- Evangelism
- Excellence
- Faith
- Family
- Fellowship
- Generosity
- Gentleness
- Godliness
- Grace
- Growth
- Honesty
- Honor
- Hope
- Humility
- Humor
- Integrity
- Justice
- Kindness
- Learning
- Loyalty
- Mercy
- Openness

- Passion
- Patience
- Perseverance
- Prayer
- Reliability
- Respect
- Sacrifice
- Selflessness
- Stewardship
- Teamwork
- Trustworthiness
- Unity
- Wisdom

Next, it's time to narrow them down. Look over your high-lighted core values and determine what five core values you believe are the most integral to your success as a leader. Grab a sharpie and underline those five core values.

Lastly, take that same sharpie, and let's find what core values we are already confident with. Write 1 through 3 on the top three core values that you feel you already hold and display well (with 1 being the strongest and 3 being the weakest).

Now that we have a better picture of what matters, you can start really attacking some goals. The easiest thing is to start with the core values that you underlined with the sharpie but did not number. These are core values that you marked as important to your success as a leader, but because you did not number them you do not feel confident in your abilities.

By completing this exercise, you've already displayed some humility and honesty with yourself. I challenge you to ask some members of your team to complete this same task regarding your leadership. You'd be amazed how much grace your team will lend you when you're intentionally working to improve your leadership skills.

Compassion

Compassion- *noun*
   sympathetic pity and concern for the sufferings or misfortunes of others.

Compassion is important so that leaders are relatable to their followers. This core value allows leaders to better connect with their followers. When people feel that they are being listened to and that their concerns are important, they are more likely to be supportive of their leader. Leaders who can show compassion successfully can help to create a more positive and productive work environment.

A study in 2014 found that employees who were exposed to unsupportive managers had lower job satisfaction and higher levels of stress. Whereas, employees who worked for supportive leaders had less burnout and higher levels of engagement.
Is there really any shock in those findings? Not only does compassion help leaders to be more productive, but it also makes them more effective.

A 2011 study found that when managers expressed compassion towards employees, the employees were happier and more motivated to do their jobs well.

I think that every single person has experienced a leader who was not compassionate. Typically, we think back on those positions as our "worst jobs ever" or that "horrible manager". As you read that, I'm sure that you thought of someone or some job that fits that description. I don't know about you, but I never want to be remembered that way. My goal is to have a positive impact on the teams that I lead and develop other strong and capable leaders. I hope that those I lead outgrow me and accomplish things that change the world.

When I was in competitive cheerleading, compassion is not a core value that I displayed for my team. I was harsh, competitive, and immovable when times got tough or our team was struggling. If I had shown more compassion to my team, I could have made a bigger impact on my teammates. I would have maintained stronger relationships with those teammates. I look around me now, and I was unable to keep a single relationship from that time in my life. I can blame only one person for that. Myself. I chose to not grow, learn and love the people around me as they deserved.

Compassionate people can think about what other people are going through and how they feel. This empathy makes a person a good leader, in part because they can put themselves in someone else's shoes. Compassionate leaders typically feel a stronger sense of confidence and purpose. When I look at the teams that I lead now, I am much more intentional about leading with compassion and love first. Remember, I only lead hard when I've been given specific permission for that individual situation with that particular person. I want my team to allow me to lead them for years, even if they move on with their careers. I'm in leadership for the long haul, not a short goal.

What about you?

What are your leadership goals?

Can you think of a time when you could've led with more compassion?

If you had reacted with compassion first, what do you think that outcome could have been?

Moving forward, do you think it would be worth an intentional effort to lead with compassion even if it takes more time or patience on your part?

Compassion is an important part of leadership in any social or team setting. This core leadership value allows for honest relationships to form more easily between the leader and their team, allowing for good communication when needed. It also shows that leaders aren't afraid to show some heart and expose their own vulnerabilities while still leading. Showing compassion will make it easier to motivate and engage with team members and co-workers, especially when everyone feels supported. Teams tend to perform better on their tasks when they feel supported by their leaders, which will reflect positively on the organization.

Listen attentively and show that you care about what they are saying. One of the best methods to display attentiveness is to repeat the summary of the statement. For instance; an employee comes to you and says that they are frustrated by the change in deadline on the reports that are due. They feel it is not enough time to get the scope of work done. An attentive leader might respond, **"I understand how important accurate work is for you. What steps can we take in the future to ensure that you have the proper time to complete the scope of work without causing this stress for you?"**

When people feel that they are being listened to and that their concerns are important, they are more likely to be supportive of the leader. Make an effort to understand their point of view. One of the best things that you can do for your employees and team is to ask yourself, **"How could I have helped create more success?"** Compassionately looking at situations through the lens of those you're leading can help to improve processes. These small adjustments will shock you with massive organizational growth.

Praise team members for good work, thank them for their efforts and let them know that you value them as people. Your team will also feel better about themselves and you as their leader when they feel appreciated by you. It is important to remember to encourage team members even when goals are not hit. Dive deeper than the surface.

Was the goal not hit because of a staffing issue, a leadership issue, or a system issue?

Was there something that you as the leader could have done to improve the odds of hitting the goal?

Could you sit down as a team and gather feedback about

what happened to create solutions as a group?

Be supportive and understanding, even when things don't go as planned. People tend to be more motivated when they think that their leader cares about them as a person rather than just seeing them as a cog in the organizational machine. A compassionate leader can help his or her team members see themselves as valuable and important, which in turn makes them more likely to work hard and perform better. Be a positive role model for your team by finding ways to ease conflict and instill harmony into an organization.

When leading a team, it is important to show compassion not just through words, but through actions as well. This means being understanding and supportive when things don't go as planned and being willing to help out when needed. It also means taking the time to listen to your team and address their concerns. Acknowledge their feelings, even when you don't agree with them. This shows that you care and that you are willing to listen. It can also help to resolve the issue faster. Incorporate compassion into your everyday life by asking people how they are doing and taking the time to truly listen to their responses.

Help your team when they need it, without judgment or criticism. As the leader, part of your job is to step up and fill in the gaps within the organization when "chips are on the table." When someone comes to you for help, be sure to offer it compassionately and without criticism. This will make them feel more comfortable and likely to come to you again in the future. It can also help to resolve any issues that may be going on. It is better to be faced with the issue than ignore it. If your team doesn't feel they can come to you with issues, it will create holes in your organization and productivity will seep out of them little by little.

I had an agent once that had lost their mother to a tragedy. They knew that the insurance job would be hard as they would have to discuss death every day for a living. They also knew that it was a passion of theirs to help families to make sure they were protected and taken care of on the worst day of their lives. This agent also had never been in a sales career before. I tried to be as understanding as I could and gave the agent extra praises to make sure they knew how proud I was of them. I failed this person in compassion though. I should have seen what the stress was doing to them and allowed them more time off throughout the week or more breaks throughout the day. Finally, the breaking point happened and the agent had a series of mini strokes in the office. Thankfully, we were able to keep them safe and get them to the hospital. I lost the agent to another company who was willing to be more compassionate about their situation. I apologized to the agent and we still speak every once in a while. They are doing great at their new company and I could not be more proud. I lost a great agent and person because I did not lead from a place of compassion first.

Empower those who need your support by helping them learn from their mistakes. Take the time to build a relationship of trust with your followers. Trust is an important factor in any relationship, and it is especially important when leading a team. When followers trust their leader, they are more likely to follow their directions and be supportive. Leaders should take the time to build a relationship of trust with their followers. This can be done by being understanding and supportive when things don't go as planned, and by being willing to help out when needed. Foster relationships with those around you by being an approachable leader. Empower those who need your support by helping them learn from their mistakes.

Communication & Storytelling

Communication: *noun*
  the successful conveying or sharing of ideas and feelings.

Storytelling: *noun*
  the activity of telling or writing stories.

Leaders are often faced with the responsibility of conveying complex ideas and concepts to their teams. They must do so in a way that is easily understood and relatable. Using storytelling is one of their most powerful tools to accomplish this. Leaders who are good communicators not only have an easier time leading others, but they also can make better decisions because of it. In this way, communication and storytelling skills are essential for anyone in a leadership role.

Storytelling is also a great way to illustrate abstract concepts. For example, if a leader wants to talk about change, they could tell the story of the phoenix rising from the ashes. This story is a perfect metaphor for change, as it illustrates the idea of rebirth and resurrection. It also has universal appeal, meaning that everyone can relate to it in some way.

Leaders who are good communicators know the importance of using storytelling to simplify complex ideas and concepts. Not only is it an effective way to communicate, but it is also a powerful tool for building relationships and inspiring others. In a world that is constantly changing, good communication and storytelling skills are more important than ever.

When I was first promoted to a leadership position in a professional setting, I didn't take into consideration the costs that my communication could have on the organization. I spoke to everyone the same, encouraged everyone the same, and treated everyone the same. This meant that I was only half as effective as I could have been. Some of my agents responded well to my communication style while half of my team couldn't stand it. I hadn't learned how to effectively communicate with people with different learning styles yet. Storytelling was not a technique that I had learned or even thought was important. There are so many effective communicators in leadership to learn from.

One leader who had excellent communication skills was Steve Jobs. He was known for his ability to simplify complex ideas and communicate them in a way that everyone could understand. He was also a great storyteller. This helped him illustrate his ideas in a way that was memorable and engaging. Jobs was able to inspire others and build a wildly successful business. Think about how difficult it must have been to communicate his vision of products that didn't exist with technology that wasn't even possible yet. He had to harness his communication skills to inspire hundreds and then thousands and finally millions of people to believe in his products and inventions.

Thanks to his skills in communication and storytelling, Jobs was able to achieve incredible things and change the world. He was a master of communication, and his skills continue to be an inspiration to leaders around the world even in his absence. Leaders can learn a lot from him about the importance of communication and how to use storytelling to illustrate their ideas. Good communication and storytelling skills are essential for anyone in a leadership role, and they can be used to achieve great things. There is a commonality in leaders with exceptional communication skills; their ideas, stories, and legacies live on even after they've passed away.

Many great communicators throughout our history changed the world as we know it by effectively communicating their beliefs to those that were around them. One of the most influential leaders and a communication model for many is Jesus. Whether you are religious or not, you can agree that you've heard at least one parable that was told by Jesus. That means that His communication style was so effective that even people outside of His sphere of influence.

Jesus was a great storyteller, and He used storytelling to illustrate His ideas in a way that was memorable and engaging. His stories were often about everyday people and events, and they were told in a way that everyone could understand. Jesus knew the importance of communication and storytelling skills, and he used them to build relationships and inspire others. Another thing to note about how Jesus communicated His stories was he would illustrate the same principle with several stories in a row. He understood that everyone communicates differently and He would need several variations to ensure that everyone would be able to grasp the lesson He was teaching.

One of Jesus' most famous stories is the parable of the prodigal son. This story is about a young man who leaves home and squanders his inheritance on wild living. Meanwhile, his brother stays at home with the father, takes care of the estate, and is responsible. When the prodigal son runs out of money, he returns home to his father. His father welcomes him with open arms rather than shunning him away. The responsible brother questions this forgiveness that the father showed to the prodigal son. The father explains that he welcomes back the son because he was lost. There is always cause to celebrate when someone who is lost is found again. Jesus used this story as an illustration of God's love and forgiveness. Jesus was a master of communication and His skills continue to be an inspiration to leaders around the world. Leaders can learn a lot from Him about the importance of communication and how to use storytelling to illustrate their ideas.

When you study great communicators, you'll realize that they communicate their ideas and thoughts in several different ways. You must realize those you lead will have different learning styles. You must be able to adjust your communication methods to reach everyone in the most effective way possible. When you think about it, the ability to communicate complex ideas and thoughts through storytelling is a powerful tool. Communication has the power to tear down an organization or build it up.

Let's look at a few communicators who had the opposite effect; Adolf Hitler (the orator), Benito Mussolini (the journalist), Joseph Stalin (the propagandist), and Kim Jong IL (the showman). I think you get the point. All of these leaders had very effective communication styles, but unfortunately, they chose to use their skills for destruction. That might seem like a giant leap, but our words have power. They either have the power to build up people and empower them to become better or they have the power to destroy those around us and encourage immoral decisions. Your communication will create the environment you live in and the culture of your organization.

On the other side of the coin, we have individuals such as Martin Luther King Jr. (the preacher), Mahatma Gandhi (the philosopher), Nelson Mandela (the negotiator), and John F. Kennedy (the idealist). These were all great communicators because they could tap into the emotional side of people and inspire them to take action.

If you look at these leaders, they all have their style and they all became known for their specific genre and style of communication. Get to know your own style of communication and work to master that technique as best you can. Just as important as it is to be a good communicator, it is also essential to be a good listener. Listening allows you to understand the other person's point of view and shows that you are interested in what they have to say. It also allows you to build relationships with the people you lead. If you cannot listen, you cannot communicate effectively, which means that you cannot lead. It's as simple as that.

Do you find yourself constantly repeating ideas or instructions to your team?

Does your team seem disengaged when you are speaking?

What is one small change that you can make with your communication to increase your effectiveness?

Do you need to change your tone of voice?

I would encourage you to also get some honest feedback from your team so that you can know where you can make small adjustments that make a big impact. Keep making small adjustments and eventually, you'll look back over time and realize the difference that you've made for the organization and how much stronger your team is for the growth that you've practiced.

Sacrifice

Sacrifice: *noun*
  an act of giving up something valued for the sake of something else regarded as more important or worthy.

As a leader, you must be willing to sacrifice things for the betterment of the organization and the people you lead. This will most likely include making personal sacrifices, such as giving up time with family and friends or sacrificing resources, such as financial investments. Leaders who can make these types of sacrifices demonstrate a strong commitment to their team and organization.

Of course, there are limits to what a leader should be willing to sacrifice. Some things should never be compromised, such as one's ethics, values, and integrity. Leaders must also be careful not to over-commit themselves, as this can lead to fatigue and burnout. Ultimately, being willing to sacrifice is a sign of strength and selflessness. It shows that the leader is dedicated to the success of the team and is willing to do whatever it takes to achieve that goal. Sacrificing is one of the most important things a leader can do for their team.

Some leaders won't ask their employees to do anything they're unwilling to do themselves. They understand that by following this philosophy, they'll be able to inspire everyone around them to work just as hard as they do. It also helps empower their teams to know that the task being asked of them is possible. Leaders need to put their organization and its members first and be willing to make decisions that may not be popular but are in the team's best interest.

One leader who has always been willing to sacrifice for his followers is Martin Luther King Jr. He was willing to give up his own time, resources, and even his safety for the sake of the civil rights movement he led. He knew that it would be a long and difficult journey, but he was committed to seeing it through. King's dedication to his cause is an example of what a leader should be willing to sacrifice for their team. He was willing to make personal sacrifices, such as giving up time with family and friends, and he was also willing to put the needs of others before his own. This type of selflessness is inspiring and motivating for team members. It builds trust and shows that the leader is looking out for their best interests.

Another leader who has always been willing to sacrifice for their followers is Mahatma Gandhi. He was willing to give up his own time, resources, and even his safety for the sake of the Indian independence movement. He knew that it would be a long and difficult journey, but he was committed to seeing it through. Gandhi's dedication to his cause is an example of what a leader should be willing to sacrifice for their team. This type of selflessness is inspiring and motivating for team members.

Both King and Gandhi are examples of leaders who under-stood that it's important to lead by example, and by doing so, they were able to inspire everyone around them to work in unison towards common goals. By doing so, leaders can inspire everyone around them to work just as hard as they do.

I can think of several times as a leader when a sacrifice was needed. It's important as the leader to remember that it's not about you. The decisions you make cannot be about you, but rather, need to be team-focused. As a new leader, I made decisions thinking only of how they affected me rather than how does it affect the team. Decisions that are as simple as adjusting the working hours, changing software systems, or updating how you track the business's revenue. These decisions can have a massive ripple effect throughout your organization.

I remember when I gained my leadership position, I immediately changed the software to one that I preferred. I thought it was the right decision to make because the software was easier for me to use. It didn't even cross my mind that revenue would be lost as we trained the other members on the team to use the new system. Because of this selfish decision, I put our organization behind hitting our goals by months. In the end, we switched back to the software that was easiest for the entire team to use because it wasn't about me. The progress of the team and the revenue of the organization were more important than my individual preferences.

Throughout my leadership role, I was determined to be the first in the door and the last out. I wanted my team to know that I was willing to sacrifice time with my family to hit our goals. They needed to trust that I would be there. They needed to see that I was willing to get into the weeds with them. This created an unbreakable bond. When I switched companies, all of my team made the switch with me without even being asked. That is a loyalty you can take to the bank.

When is a time that you made a decision that negatively affected your organization?

Was this decision one that could have been approached differently for a more positive outcome?

Did you make the decision out of selfishness or selflessness?

It might seem easy to pinpoint decisions that we've made in the past that were selfish, but the goal is to recognize selfish decisions before making them. You should always try to lead with sacrifice first. It is much more difficult than it seems because by human nature we are selfish. Being selfish occasionally is not a cause for defeat. Just call it out, change directions, apologize if necessary, and move on.

Generosity

Generosity: *noun*
the quality of being kind and generous.

A generous leader is someone always willing to give more than they take. They are always looking for ways to help out their team, and they are always willing to share their resources. As a result, they typically see greater results from their team. One of the biggest benefits of being a generous leader is that it builds trust.

Do you see the recurring theme with these leadership traits?

When team members know that their leader is always looking out for their best interests, they will be more likely to trust them. This can lead to better communication and more productive teams. Another benefit of being a generous leader is that it helps create a positive work environment. Team members who feel appreciated by their leader, are going to be more motivated to do their best. This most often will lead to better performance and more productive teams.

I've been asked several times from individuals higher than me in organizations, **"Why does your team stick around even when they aren't closing sales?"** The simplest answer that I can give them is that I've gained my team's trust through generosity. My main goal with my team is to not micromanage them for success but to empower them to create their own.

This can mean slower growth, but I'd take growth that sticks over the quick success that dissipates quickly. Think about how much time you are wasting constantly training new people to replace the team members that you lost. I know that when I pour knowledge, love, and time into my team, they will be around for me to see the seeds that I'm planting grow.

One example of a generous leader is Oprah Winfrey. Oprah has been a generous leader throughout her career, and she has been able to achieve great results because of it. As a result, she has built a strong following of loyal fans. Oprah has also been able to create a positive work environment, and her team is known for being highly productive. Oprah Winfrey's generosity led her to create the Oprah Winfrey Leadership Academy for Girls. This academy provides high-quality education to disadvantaged girls from all over the world. Oprah has also given millions of dollars to charity and supported numerous other causes. As a result, she has become one of the most philanthropic celebrities in the world.

Warren Buffett is another example of a generous leader. Buffett has donated billions of dollars to charity throughout his career. He has become one of the most recognized names in the world. One of Buffett's biggest donations was his donation of $37 billion to the Gates Foundation. This donation was the largest in history, and it helped support the Foundation's goal of improving education and health around the world. Buffett has also been generous with his time, and he has given many lectures on philanthropy. As a result, he has inspired other people to give back to their communities.

One thing that you'll recognize when you compare generous leaders; they seem to always be successful. It seems the opposite of what should happen to people who give away so much of their time and money. I believe that we are rewarded by our generosity with even more success. It manifests that you are trustworthy to steward more.

When you can be trusted with little, you'll be given even more.

Let's think about it with the tithe. My husband and I tithe 10% of our income every week to our church. We do this because we feel it is our duty to the church. This generosity should put us 10% behind on our bills or the things we want to do with our money. However, each time that we tithe, it seems that we have that money magically (or spiritually) replaced plus some. This is our reward for being trustworthy, generous stewards of what we've been given.

I try and treat my team the same way. I've been trusted to steward the growth of these individuals and ensure they each achieve their success. It is not my job to define what their success is or force them to achieve it. My job is to be a resource and pour everything I have into the individuals who are ready and asking to receive it.

It comes down to intention.

If I want to be a generous leader and I set a goal of being generous each day, I will likely achieve that to varying degrees daily. If I want to be a generous leader, but constantly make decisions without regard for other people or push my objectives on my team, I likely won't build the trust I'm looking for. If I walk around believing that I am a money magnet and I will be provided for, I will likely always have opportunity knocking. If I walk around feeling pity for myself and the state of my income, I will likely be disappointed by my checking account balance and net worth.

Isaac Newton said, **"Things that stay in motion tend to stay in motion."** If we want to be successful and see greater results, we need to be generous leaders who are always in motion. We need to give more than we take, help others achieve their goals, and be a positive force in the world. When we do this, our team will respond with productivity and loyalty. We'll also see greater success in our own lives.

Generosity is one of the defining traits of a great leader. Generous leaders typically see greater results from their teams. This is because generosity inspires trust and builds relationships. When team members feel that their leader cares about them, they are more likely to be loyal and productive. Finally, being a generous leader can also help you attract top talent. Talented employees want to work for leaders who are going to help them grow and develop. By being a generous leader, you can show potential employees that you are serious about helping them reach their goals.

What are some things that you can do to become a more generous leader?

1. Set a goal to be generous each day.
2. Help team members achieve their own success.
3. Be a positive force in the world.
4. Attract top talent by being generous with your time

Evangelism

Evangelism: *noun*
    zealous advocacy of a cause.

Evangelistic leaders tend to have more success than greedy leaders. Greedy leaders are focused on themselves and their enrichment, while evangelistic leaders are focused on helping others learn about and follow Jesus Christ. I believe a great contributor to this is the focus. Remember what we learned about mission-focused leaders. Evangelical leaders typically have a focus on their passions and efforts to make a difference in the world. This focus typically aids in them being more specifically focused as their goals are centered around their larger mission.

Evangelism is the preaching of the gospel. It is the proclamation of the good news that Jesus Christ died for our sins and rose from the dead. Evangelism is an essential part of the Christian life. We are called to share the gospel with those who are lost and need to hear the good news. Jesus Christ said, **"Go into all the world and preach the gospel to all creation" (Mark 16:15).** He also said, **"And this gospel of the kingdom**

will be preached in the whole world as a testimony to all nations, and then the end will come" (Matthew 24:14).

Greedy leaders, on the other hand, are focused on themselves and their own enrichment. This focus leads them to be more self-centered in all areas of their lives including business. The difference in focus is also evident in the way that the two types of leaders treat those around them. Evangelical leaders typically have greater success in building relationships with others. They want to help others grow and learn. Greedy leaders, on the other hand, typically have a focus on taking advantage of relationships with others. Their relationships hinge on them getting something from them rather than contributing.

Greedy leaders often mistreat those who work for them or who are under their authority. They may demand excessive amounts of work from their employees, or take advantage of them in other ways. Evangelistic leaders, on the other hand, often go out of their way to help those around them. They may share their wealth with those who are less fortunate, or they may assist those who are struggling.

I'll give you an example of a greedy leader. A few years ago, I worked for a company that was run by greedy leaders. These leaders were focused on themselves and their own enrichment. They demanded excessive amounts of work from their employees and showed no interest in their team's growth. They were not interested in building relationships with others, and they mistreated those who worked for them. As a result, the company was in a constant state of turmoil. The employees were unhappy and the business was struggling. When it came down to the wire, all the employees chose to leave the company high and dry. This created a gap in the organization and put them at least three years our from hitting their revenue goals.

Now, these leaders believed that they were going to make an impact. They were successful there. Unfortunately, their impact was negative because of their treatment of their staff. Cutting corners to pad their pocket had the opposite effect. If they had been more evangelical, they would have had better treatment of the team which would have increased production and helped them hit their revenue goals. Sometimes this is slower growth than we'd like, but it's more impactful and long-term growth. I'd take that any day.

An example of an evangelistic leader is my pastor. He is focused on helping others learn about and follow Jesus Christ. He builds genuine relationships with his congregation and the other leaders within the church. He is not interested in taking advantage of others for his benefit. As a result, the church is in a constant state of growth. The congregation is happy and the church is thriving. They have grown from the church renting a garage to now having over 24 locations and are located in over 7 states.

My family and I attend Life Church. This church has accomplished amazing feats with the help of God moving their needle when they reach their limitations. Life Church is the creator and steward of the Bible App. It has almost one billion downloads. The church offers the Youversion app 100% free around the world so they can help as many people gain access to the word of God. Life Church and Pastor Craig Groeschel are great examples of how evangelism is rewarded. Remember, when you can be trusted with little, you will be given much.

The Bible tells us that we are called to evangelize the world. It is our responsibility to share the gospel with those who are lost and need to hear the good news. We should not be afraid to share the gospel with others. We should also be willing to put our lives on the line for the sake of the gospel. The apostle Paul said, **"For I am not ashamed of the gospel, because it is the power of God that brings salvation to everyone who believes: first to the Jew, then to the Gentile" (Romans 1:16)**.

One of the ways that I've incorporated my faith into my business is by sharing a verse each day. I customize the verse to make it relevant to the business. I follow it up with examples or stories about how it relates to our organization. I also share the verse of the day on my Facebook story. This allows the people who want to see it access but can be avoided by those that are opposed. I don't force-feed my religion on anyone, but I find that the Bible has the perfect business plan written out in it if you're willing to look for it. I've seen great success in my business and growth in my leadership by studying the lessons in the Bible. I believe that I should offer the word of God in a pressure-free environment to as many people as possible.

It took me years to get there and I wish I'd be more willing to share sooner. Now, I have members of my team who complete Bible study plans with me regarding leadership, business plans, and relationship building. This helps to increase the footprint of my organization by building up other leaders instead of keeping it all to myself. It also helps us to build long-term genuine, positive relationships with each other. I've had some agents move into a new career path and we still stay in contact because of the relationship that we formed during their time with me. When it comes down to it, evangelistic leaders have a much greater impact on the world than greedy leaders do. Greedy leaders may be successful in the short term, but they ultimately fail in their efforts to make a lasting difference.

Billy Graham is a popular evangelistic leader who has had a

tremendous impact on the world. He has preached the gospel all over the world, and he has been a powerful witness for Christ. He is a man of integrity and compassion, and he has dedicated his life to proclaiming the good news of Jesus Christ. Billy Graham is a true ambassador for Christ, and his ministry has touched the lives of millions of people.

Another evangelistic leader is Matthew McConaughey. He is a popular actor who has also been involved in evangelism. He has spoken about his faith on numerous occasions, and he has shared the gospel with many people. He is a passionate evangelist, and he is committed to sharing the good news of Jesus Christ with as many people as possible. Matthew McConaughey is a great example of an evangelistic leader because has a passion for the gospel, and he is devoted to sharing the good news with others. He has attributed much of his success to his belief system and God blessing him with a larger audience by the platform he has been placed on.

Evangelism is an essential part of leadership. Leaders who are focused on evangelism have a greater impact on the world than those who are not. Evangelistic leaders are dedicated to reaching the lost, and they are willing to do whatever it takes to share the good news of Jesus Christ. As a leader, I am given a platform of influence and I must use that platform to the best of my abilities. For me, that includes spreading my faith.

I have a challenge for you.

1. Write a brief sentence or paragraph about where you are right now.
2. Write a brief sentence or paragraph about where you want to be.

3. Choose one way that you can share your faith in your business.
4. Be intentional about doing that thing each day.
5. Every day, thank God for what you have written down in step one.
6. Every day, pray that God helps take you to what you wrote down in step two.

Do this for 90 days straight and watch God work. He loves showing off his power and might. Give him the stage to put on a display of his support for your success.

Love

Love: *noun*
an intense feeling of deep affection.

No one can deny that being a leader is a difficult job. But it's also a very rewarding one. One of the most important aspects of being a successful leader is showing love and appreciation to those who follow them. When people feel appreciated, they're more likely to be dedicated and loyal to their leader. Leaders who don't show love and appreciation to their followers usually don't see as much success. This is because a lack of love creates a disconnection between the leader and the team. When this happens, the team members are less likely to be motivated and inspired to do their best. Showing love is not always easy, but it's definitely worth the effort.

Leaders should express gratitude regularly.

Thanking your team for their hard work and dedication will create leaps and bounds in productivity. Let them know that you appreciate everything they do to help the organization succeed. There are several ways for you to show your gratitude. Thank your team immediately after they do something helpful. You don't have to make a big show out of gratitude. It can be the simple, private expressions of gratitude that make the biggest impact. A simple, **"Thank you for your hard work today,"** could be just the statement an employee needs to show up one more day. **"I really appreciate how helpful you are,"** might bring in that extra push you needed from your team. If you're not comfortable with verbal appreciation, get started by writing some simple cards, notes, or emails to your team.

A great way to show appreciation is by giving your team a gift or taking them out for dinner. This not only shows appreciation, but it helps the team to bond. When your team feels connected, it is more likely for them to work together as a team on their projects. One of my favorite sayings is **"if you want to go fast, go alone. If you want to go far, go with others."**

Some of your team members will need acknowledgment of their accomplishments. Each member of your team will likely have a different communication style. In relationships, we call it "love language". In a workplace, it is similar but without romance. For members of your team that need to be affirmed, recognition of their contributions and accomplishments to the group will be very influential. Remember, that having to learn to communicate in a way that is uncomfortable to you is a likely sacrifice you will need to make for your team.

A fantastic tool for showing love is to take an actual interest in their lives. I've made it a point to ensure that my team can come to me with anything. I want to know what's going on in their lives. I want to know how their family is. I want to know how they are doing. It requires that I genuinely care about my team, but also it does help the organization to hit its production goals. This love that I show my team has resulted in loyalty and support beyond what I ever thought I had earned.

> Leaders should be supportive and offer encourage-
> ment and positive feedback.

Let your followers know that you believe in them and that you support their efforts. Offer words of encouragement, and be there to help pick them up when they fall. When things go wrong, a leader's priority should be to take care of their team. Offer support, sympathy, and understanding. Do whatever you can to help your team members feel better. Leaders who show love are often successful in maintaining a positive relationship with their teams. When people feel appreciated and loved, they are more likely to be dedicated and loyal to their leader. Leaders who don't show love and appreciation to their followers usually don't see much success. This is because a lack of love creates a disconnection between the leader and the followers. When this happens, the followers are less likely to be supportive and more likely to be uncooperative.

> Showing love is a critical part of being a successful
> leader.

Love isn't always easy to show, but it's definitely worth the effort. Leaders should express gratitude as regularly as possible. It's important to show your team love when there is a failure too. Make a point to create a safe environment for failures. Remember, the only failure is not trying at all. When you show love even through failure, you empower your team to try new things, techniques, and strategies. Who knows, you might just find a new ingenious process because a team member takes a chance and tries something new. Leaders who show love are often successful in maintaining a positive relationship with their teams. Above all else, a leader must be genuine. Don't just pretend to care; take an actual interest in your teams' lives and concerns. Build relationships of trust and mutual respect.

One leader who showed love to their followers was Dr. Martin Luther King Jr. He was a leader who cared about his followers and was always there to offer words of encouragement. He showed his followers that he believed in them and supported their efforts. Dr. Martin Luther King Jr. was a great example of a leader who showed love to his followers. Look how far and wide his influence was able to go because of the love he showed to his followers. His mission has traveled through generations because of the love and empowerment he showed.

One leader who didn't show love to their followers was Kim Jong-un. He was a leader who cared about himself and his own goals, and he didn't really care about his followers. He was often unsupportive and uncooperative. The outcome of Kim Jong-un's leadership continues to be disastrous. He shows no remorse or pause for his decisions. Thousands of his followers flee his country every year because of his leadership practices.

Leaders who show love are often successful in maintaining a positive relationship with their followers. Am I beating a dead horse yet? While it's not always easy, leaders should make an effort to show love and appreciation to those they lead. It's definitely worth the effort.

Are you showing the love to your team that you should be?

Are you guilty of showing love only to those people who you believe deserve it?

What is one small step you can take in a more positive direction?

Who is someone you look up to that has always shown you love, even through your mistakes?

What is a specific thing you can emulate from how they showed you love?

Servitude

Servitude: *noun*
    the state of being a slave or completely subject to
    someone or something.

To build loyalty among their team members, leaders need to show servitude. Sacrifice is similar, but they are not the same. By definition, servitude is the state of being a servant. Sacrifice is regarding individual decisions. Servitude is a constant state. In a business setting, this means that leaders should be willing to do whatever it takes to help their team members succeed.

Ultimately, team members need to feel like their leader is invested in their success full-time. By showing servitude, leaders can build loyalty and trust. Loyalty is a two-way street with relationships. It should never be a one-sided transaction. If you expect loyalty and service from your team, you must first be willing to give them both.

Some ways that leaders can show servitude include:

- Making themselves available to help team members with

whatever they need
- Picking up slack when someone is struggling
- Offering advice and mentorship
- Running out and grabbing the lunch so your team can maintain momentum
- Offering guidance and advice when team members need it
- Putting the team's success before their personal goals
- Going above and beyond to help the team succeed

To make themselves available to their teams, leaders need to be accessible to help team members with whatever they need, putting the team's success before their own goals and going above and beyond to help the team succeed. This means that they should be willing to meet with team members whenever they need to and be available for questions.

Leaders can also make themselves available by being active on social media and other online platforms. This allows team members to communicate with leaders easily and without having to schedule a meeting. Leaders should offer guidance to their team members whenever they need it. Offering guidance shows that the leader is invested in the team's success. Leaders can give guidance in a variety of ways, including through mentorship, coaching, and training. By mentoring team members, leaders can help them learn from their own experiences and mistakes. Coaching team members allows leaders to give specific and actionable feedback, which can help team members improve their skills. Training team members help them learn the ropes of their job and become familiar with the company's procedures. The guidance doesn't always have to be a formal process to be effective. Team members will begin to grow and develop professionally when they are closely connected to a strong leader.

One great example of a leader who went above and beyond to help their team succeed is Martin Luther King Jr. After being arrested for his role in the Montgomery Bus Boycott, King was released on bail. He then traveled to St. Louis, where he delivered a speech on racism and segregation. The following day, he flew to New York City to meet with President Dwight Eisenhower. Despite his busy schedule, King continued to work tirelessly for the success of the Civil Rights Movement. He gave speeches, organized protests, and met with political leaders to bring about change. His dedication and commitment to his team helped spur one of the most successful social movements in history.

King's example shows that leaders need to be willing to go above and beyond for their team to see success. By being available and making sacrifices, King was able to help the Civil Rights Movement achieve great things. Leaders can learn a lot from his example and apply it to their own teams.

Aly Raisman, the captain of the U.S. women's gymnastic Olympic team in 2012 and 2016, is another great example of a leader who put her team before herself. She was dedicated to the success of her team and did everything she could to help them win. Raisman went above and beyond for her team by consistently working hard in practice and giving it her all during competitions. She was also very supportive of her teammates, always cheering them on and helping them to stay positive. Raisman's dedication to her team helped them to achieve great things, including winning the gold medal at the 2012 Olympic Games.

> Leaders can use their example to inspire their team to greatness.

Raisman not only went above and beyond for her team during competition but helped lead her team to a successful guilty verdict of her gymnastics coach. In the summer of 2017, Aly Raisman's gymnastics coach was charged with sexual assault. Raisman immediately came forward to support her teammates and help them through a tough time. She publicly testified in court against her coach and helped ensure that he would be punished for his crimes. Raisman's example shows that leaders need to be there for their team members in times of need. By standing up for her teammates and helping them through a difficult time, Raisman demonstrated the importance of servitude. Leaders can learn from her example and do their best to provide support for their team when needed.

What is stopping you from serving in extraordinary ways just like these leaders?

In what ways could you step up and serve your team to a greater capacity?

Think of a specific instance where your lack of servitude had a negative effect on our team?

Now, take that same situation and predict what would have happened had you led as a servant leader.

What does that look like?

Solitude

> Solitude: *noun*
> the state or situation of being alone.

Leaders are constantly under pressure to make decisions and keep their teams moving forward. However, it's important to take time to re-energize. This can be done through solitude. Being alone can help you reflect on your thoughts and feelings, which is beneficial when you need to make tough decisions. It also allows for recharging your batteries so you can be more effective when leading.

However, leaders shouldn't stay in solitude for too long. They need to balance their time between being alone and being with others. If they spend too much time alone, they may become isolated and out of touch with what's going on around them. But if they spend too much time with others, they may not have enough time to reflect on their thoughts. Finding the right balance is key for leaders when it comes to solitude. Solitude is something that every leader should make time for regularly. There are several positive activities that leaders can do to re-energize themselves. Some of these activities include exercise, meditation, and spending time in nature.

Exercise is a great way to release energy and stress.

It helps to rid any negative feelings and maintain focus. Meditation is another activity that can clear minds and recharge. It allows time to focus on breathing and being intentionally present in the moment. Lastly, spending time in nature can also be beneficial for leaders. Being in nature allows relaxation and taking in the beauty creates a calming space for reflection.

All of these activities are great ways for leaders to re-energize themselves. They can help leaders clear their minds, release stress, and focus on what's important. When leaders take the time to do these activities, they'll be able to lead their team more effectively. Leaders often have a lot of stress and responsibilities on their plate. This can be a lot to handle, and leaders need to find ways to manage this stress.

What are you currently using to de-stress and recharge?

One way to do this is through therapy. Therapy can be beneficial for leaders because it allows them to talk about their thoughts and feelings in a safe and confidential space. This can help manage stress and anxiety. It can also help leaders learn more about themselves and how they react to certain situations. This self-awareness can help make better decisions. Therapy can also help leaders develop healthy coping mechanisms for when they're feeling overwhelmed. This can be beneficial in the long run, as it can help leaders stay healthy and balanced. Leaders who are struggling with stress or anxiety should consider seeking out therapy. It can be a great way for them to manage their emotions and become more effective leaders.

Have you tried therapy?

If not, is it a humility issue or just something you never considered?

Mastermind groups can be a great way for leaders to connect with others and share their experiences. In a mastermind group, leaders can talk about their challenges and get feedback from others. This can help develop strategies and solutions. When leaders are around other like-minded individuals, it can be motivating and inspiring. This can help them continue to push themselves and stay focused on their goals.

Who do you have around you that would be great to create a mastermind group with?

Leaders should be constantly reading because it allows them to learn and grow. Reading allows leaders to gain new insights and knowledge that can help them in their work. They can also learn about new trends and developments in their industry. This constant practice also helps leaders stay up-to-date on the latest research. It is important, as it can help them make better decisions and stay ahead of the competition. Lastly, reading can help leaders develop a new perspective. By reading books from different genres, leaders can get a broader view of the world. This can be helpful in developing new strategies and approaches.

What are the last five books that you've read?
1.
2.
3.
4.
5.
Now, let's look at how frequently you're reading. Next to the titles you listed above, write the month and year that you read each book.

If there is more than a two-month gap between these dates, reading is something that should go to the top of your new habit list. Utilize the discipline techniques that we've discussed to create this consistency in your life.

There are many reasons why leaders should read the Bible. First and foremost, the Bible is a source of wisdom and knowledge. It contains teachings from God that can help leaders make better decisions. The Bible also contains stories about people who were successful in life. These stories can be inspiring and motivating for leaders. It has verses that leaders can use for guidance and direction. By reading it, leaders can receive God's wisdom on how to handle different situations. Lastly, the Bible is a source of comfort and hope. It contains promises from God that can help leaders through difficult times.

There are many great books in the Bible for leaders to read. One of my favorites is the book of Proverbs. This book is full of wisdom and teachings from God. Proverbs contain verses that leaders can use for guidance and direction. Another great book for leaders in the book of Psalms. This book contains Psalms, which are songs of praise and thanksgiving to God. Psalms are a great source of comfort and hope for leaders. The book of James is also a great book for leaders. In this book, James gives practical advice on how to live a faithful life. He also talks about the importance of being patient and having faith. The book of Acts is another great book for leaders. In this book, we see the story of how the early church was formed and grew. This book is a great example of how God can use people to further His Kingdom. These are just a few of the great books in the Bible for leaders. I encourage you to read all of them!

Solitude should excite you.

This is when you get to be selfish as a leader and pour back into yourself. Finally! It can be about you and what you need. You cannot give to others if you have worn yourself thin. Find the activity that helps you feel the most at peace and schedule it into your day. For me, I schedule two hours each day that are completely reserved for solitude. I like scheduling my solitude and keeping each day different. For instance; Mondays I read, Tuesdays I play the violin, Wednesdays I watch TV, Thursdays I paint, Fridays I read. I also make time to work in lunches with mastermind groups or like-minded business owners.

Take time to think about how you'd like to structure your week for solitude. Write it.

Monday Activity: From: To:
Tuesday Activity: From: To:
Wednesday Activity: From: To:
Thursday Activity: From: To:

Friday Activity: From: To:

Now, commit. Write it out on your calendar and mark yourself as busy. Take your solitude seriously.

Leading By Example

Leading: *verb*
showing (someone or something) the way to a destination by going in front of or beside them.

Example: *verb*
be illustrated or exemplified.

Good leaders must be willing to lead by example if they ever want their teams to follow. This means being willing to put in the extra effort and work, even when things are tough. It also means setting the right example for your team, being honest, and being authentic with them. If you can't do these things, it will be difficult for your team to trust you, and eventually, they will stop following you. So, if you want to be a good leader, always lead by example.

We've discussed several qualities of leadership that every leader should work on constantly to continually improve their influence abilities. I'm sure there are several qualities that you wish your team would display also. As humans, the only way that we gain new skills is by practice and modeling. The same goes for leadership qualities. The only way that your team will develop new leadership qualities is by you modeling those qualities for them.

Think about the qualities that you want your team to develop and make sure that you are exemplifying those qualities. If you want your team to be more innovative, lead by being innovative yourself. If you want your team to be better at problem-solving, lead by example and work through problems with them.

Some of the leadership qualities that you should model for your team are:

»Discipline – Always be disciplined in your actions and words. Know that your team will take their cue from you, so make sure to set a good example.

»Fight – Never give up, no matter how difficult things get. Know that there will be setbacks along the way, but don't let these stop you from reaching your goals.

»Invest – Take the time to get to know your team members on a personal level. This will help them trust you more and feel more comfortable following your lead.

»Mission-Focused – Make sure that your team knows the bigger picture and why they are doing the work they are doing. This will help them stay motivated when things get tough.

»*Humility – Be humble and admit when you are wrong. This will show your team that you are human and that they can come to you with their own mistakes.*

»*Compassion – Show compassion for your team members, even when they make mistakes. This will show them that you care about their well-being and not just their work.*

»*Communication – Make sure that you are always communicating effectively with your team. This means sharing information clearly and honestly, listening to their feedback, and being open to communication even opinions you disagree with.*

»*Sacrifice – Be willing to make sacrifices for your team, both big and small. This will show them that you are truly invested in their success.*

»*Generosity – Be generous with your time, energy, and resources. This will show your team that you are willing to give them what they need to succeed.*

»*Evangelism – Believe in your team and their abilities, and be passionate about sharing that with others. This will help them feel more confident in themselves and inspired to reach even higher.*

»*Love – Ultimately, lead with love. Love your team members for who they are, and show them that you care about their well-being. This will help them feel more connected.*

»*Servitude – Serve your team members, and put their needs above your own. This will show them that you are willing to go the extra mile for them.*

»*Solitude – Take time for yourself to reflect and rejuvenate. This will help you stay energized and focused when working with your team.*

Leadership is not easy, but it is worth it!

By leading by example, you can help your team reach their full potential and create a lasting legacy. As a leader, it's important to always be growing your skillset and perfecting your craft. One of the best ways to do this is by leading by example. If you want your team to develop new skills, you must first model those skills for them. Only then will they be able to learn and grow into the leaders you want them to be.

Conclusion

This can start to seem overwhelming, but remember that you learned to walk one step at a time. Any new skill is going to be similar. Start with the basics and then move on to more difficult concepts as you become more comfortable. And as always, practice makes perfect.

Now that you know the skills you need to grow in leadership,

Don't be a Lemon! And remember, no one wants to buy a lemon car and no one wants to follow a lemon leader.

I challenge you to share this Don't Be A Lemon with someone you think will be inspired by the actionable steps you've taken throughout this book. If you'd like to earn some money while you do it, join our affiliate program by scanning the qr code below:

AFFILIATE PROGRAM

About the Author

Channing Gardner is a shield to those that God allows her to lead. Her experience in leadership ranges from competitive sports to management positions, and leading when not in charge. She is the owner and CEO of the CG Agency in Oklahoma which specializes in helping small business owners set up employee benefits packages. Her agency includes over 45 agents nationwide working in unison toward a specific vision. She has made it a mission to learn, collect and distribute as much leadership content in an organized format as possible. The goal is to help others realize they don't have to be perfect to be an effective leader as long as they are continuously growing. Her purpose is to help others with their own personal development. Raising up other leaders is the only way to positively change your current environment or situation.

You can connect with me on:

- https://www.channinggardner.com
- https://www.facebook.com/channingegardner
- https://www.instagram.com/channingegardner
- https://range.me/yop77hXbIRWcvu5xlh77-A